KNOCKED DOWN, BUT NOT DESTROYED

JERRY MILLS

outskirts
press

It's not as I will, but as your will, Lord, because you know what's best for us better than we know ourselves. So I pray that this book will bring souls to God; this was my sole purpose for writing it. To get into a spiritual life with God, we must first be fully convicted of all our iniquities and heartfelt repentance before God in order that this change can take place. One day I read the Ten Commandments and realized I was guilty of most of them, and this stayed on my mind for a while. I knew then it was time to make a change. Once you start reading the devotions, you will see that they begin with the Ten Commandments. I hope that readers will find their way back into the arms of God. Be joyful in God, our Savior!

The way of the righteous is like the first gleam of dawn, which shines ever brighter until the full light of day. Proverbs 4:18

KNOCKED DOWN, BUT NOT DESTROYED!

I chose this title because it is a reflection of my life. I'm sure we all have been knocked around from time to time. When you think about the cause and effect, most of the damage we endure is of our own choosing. If we could just turn our negative thinking into a positive learning experience—meaning if we would pay more attention to blessings and leave the adversities to our Lord and Savior—we could smooth out a lot of bumps in the road. Do you remember the song "(Glory, Glory, Hallelujah) Since I've Laid My Burden Down"? Most people these days will first try to handle things themselves instead of laying down their burden before God. This could save you a round trip because you will return to Him!

Each page that you read will show you how God changed my life with His words. There may be some who read these pages and poke a hole in them from the beginning to the end. I would like them to remember that everyone's path is not the same, and God uses people in different ways to get His message across. My goal was to keep it simple, and if I only reach one soul, I pray that he or she would play it forward to keep the word of God moving to others. When your iniquities start making you feel shameful, you will know that your life is changing for the better. As for me, I feel like Peter when the rooster crowed. When the Lord turned and looked at him, Peter went away and wept bitterly.

This is what happens to me when I do things against the will of God. I still make mistakes, but now I don't try to fix them on my own. We all know what happens when we fight a battle without Him. God's how-to instruction manual teaches us that we may fall down, but we are not out. To God be all the glory!

In 2008, on a hot, muggy August night in Georgia, I had a massive heart attack. Let me explain what I remember about that night. The entire time I felt as if I was floating through the house and being led to the car, and I started seeing things while I was floating. I remember seeing my daughter's face, which made me feel pretty low and dismayed because I had not been in her life as a father should be, spending so much time away from her. This was when the whispers started; they were saying, "Do you remember the lifestyle that you've been living?" God actually saved my children and their mother from a great deal of heartache and possibly saved their lives. I was like an out-of-control train with no brakes headed for a steel wall. So, in 1980, I decided to join the military for a while. I thought I had shaken the devil by leaving my past behind, but what a short-lived moment that was. The evil one is never idle; his goal was to steal, kill, and destroy any joy and peace that I was trying to find.

A little before my time in the military was to end, I had an unfortunate accident while training. Who would have known that I would still be living with the pains of this incident today? Since the mid-1980s, sleep hadn't come easily because of the increasing pain, and pain pills were the only way for me to get rest. After a while, the pills weren't getting the job done, so I took them to a level that many folks don't make it back from, while trying to hide the pain and lies that I was living with. To add insult to injury, my dad was a real buddy to me while being strict when he needed to be, and he always made sure that our needs were met. I worked for him and with him from a very young age, and when there was no work, my dad, my brother, and I would go on fishing trips in Northern California. Man, did we enjoy each other's company being the only people on the lake in the mountains. Then the bad news hit our family: my dad was sick. I didn't think much about it until one day I took him to the hospital and overheard the doctors saying that there was nothing more they could do for him. This was a hard pill to swallow, and after his death, I went on a tailspin out of control, doing things that were not in line with the will of God.

One sleepless night I asked God, "Why me?" Again the whisper said to me, "Remember the way you've been living your life." I packed up my belongings, left California, and headed south. Again I thinking that I had left the devil and all my sins behind, but we can't underestimate the evil one's plan to destroy us and take away anything good that God has blessed us with. The South was no different from California. I started doing what the evil one enjoyed seeing: more sin. Once in Georgia, I started praying and reading my Bible and asking God to help me get back all that the devil had stolen from me. What a God we serve! He keeps blessing us even when we complain about our needs. This should tell us that He will not abandon those who believe. As God continued to bless me with a job at a large company, things were going well. I worked my way up to a leadership position, always trying to be the first to show up for work each morning while also trying to be a friend and team player to everyone. I made a big mistake by letting down my guard and removing the armor of God's word. It seems that some of my coworkers were battling the evil one as I was, and I often wonder if they knew that they were doing the work for the devil himself. By no means do I blame them because the whisper came to me again: "Do you remember the life you've been living?"

One Sunday night I was feeling bad, sweating with chest pains. I told my wife to take me to the hospital, and once I got into the car, it was an out-of-body experience. I woke up lying in the hospital with wires and tubes hooked up to me after a massive heart attack. I will stop and give thanks to the almighty God and my Lord and Savior because He kept me! And I give thanks to my mother, who never stopped praying for me through all the pain I caused her. I thank God that I have a praying mother. And last but not least, I give thanks to my wife who put up with me; through all the things I have done, she stayed by my side. The night she took me to the hospital and drove like she was behind the wheel of a race car, she had to run every red light and exceed the speed limit to save my life, I was told. With 40 percent of my heart functioning, all I wanted was to get back to work. Sad to say, some of my coworkers weren't feeling the same about my return. In my mind they made my job more difficult. This was not the company; it was a few who felt I stood in their way, or they didn't agree with the way I worked. Then that whisper returned, saying again, "Do you remember the life you've been living? Don't blame anyone; it is you who is in need of prayer."

This is just a short version of my story. On June 3, 2018, I went to the city in Florida where I was born and was baptized in the gulf at Port St. Joe. From this point forward I will do my best to show love as God has shown me. Yes, He kept me!

THE FIRST OF THE TEN COMMANDMENTS

"You shall have no other gods before me." If only we followed God's commandments, this world would be a better place. When I think about this commandment, I realize that as humans, at one point or another, we have put more love into a person, place, or thing than into God. Let's stop for a moment and ask ourselves, "Is there anything or anyone other than God that we allow to navigate our lives, or do we let man-made distractions take away our time from the word of God? We all fall short of this commandment. Our effort should be to make God our first love because nothing in this world can ease our pain like He can. Proverbs 3:6 says, "In all your ways acknowledge him, and he will make straight your paths." It would be unmindful and dangerous for us to place our Lord anywhere but first; He is second to none. God is the alpha and omega. What He starts, He will be there to finish—unlike humans!

THE SECOND OF THE TEN COMMANDMENTS

"You shall not make for yourself a carved image." This command goes hand in hand with the first. Idolatry is universal these days, and it doesn't have to be a carved image for those like me who need to have things simplified. This commandment refers to worshipping man-made idols. Most idol worshipping starts by observing the people you look up to most, from generation to generation. Your children will follow whatever or whomever they see you revere. "This is what the Lord says: What did your ancestors find wrong with me that led them to stray so far from me? They worshipped worthless idols, only to become worthless themselves" (Jeremiah 2:5). Our God is a jealous God, but don't get it twisted. God's jealousy is pure and holy, unlike humans, whose jealousy contains envy and sometimes evil. When you find yourself leaning to give praise to any idols, ask the Holy Spirit to take control and shatter any idols that your flesh may crave. Memorize this truth: You shall have no other gods before me. Amen.

THE THIRD OF THE TEN COMMANDMENTS

"You shall not take the name of the Lord your God in vain, for the Lord will not hold him guiltless who takes his name in vain." This literally means to alter who God is and what He stands for. If we are believers of the Gospel and give a false account of God in our sin, we have broken this commandment. How many times have you said, "I swear to God," as if this made you righteous by using God's name in a plan that He should have no part in? Keep in mind that no one in this world is righteous—no, not one—when using the Lord God's name. We should follow Jesus's example; Jesus did justice to His name by never taking His Father's name in an unavailing effort at any time. There are many ways to break this commandment, but one way to keep it is to ask yourself what Jesus would do or say before you spit out any words. Also, remember the best of men are men at best! Amen.

THE FOURTH OF THE TEN COMMANDMENTS

"Remember the Sabbath day, to keep it holy." You have six days each week for regular work, but the seventh day is a Sabbath day of rest dedicated to the Lord your God. I understand what God is saying, but the confusion comes from humans with their adjustments to God's word. Some obligations make it difficult to keep the Sabbath day, and different congregations have set their own day. After some homework, I learned that the church had good reasons to change the Sabbath from the seventh day of the week to the first day of the week. It decided that the Sabbath could no longer be referenced without acknowledging the work of Christ Jesus, and on the first day of the week, Jesus was raised for our justification. The Son of man is Lord even of the Sabbath and should be praised all day, every day, for His sacrifice. Our job is to keep the word of God and not make adjustments to it or act as if we know more than Christ Jesus. How can a mere mortal, who is not only foolish but also sinful, question or change the laws of the almighty God! Amen.

THE FIFTH OF THE TEN COMMANDMENTS

"Honor your father and mother." This commandment, I think, is one that everyone is guilty of not following, except for Christ Jesus. At some point in our lives, we have said or done something that would not show honor to our parents, and these days we find an excuse for every sin. God did not say honor them only if they didn't make a mistake; it says honor your father and mother with nothing added. To honor them is to appreciate them, accept their authority, and treat them with respect. Your father and mother come second only to God and your spouse, no one and nothing else. Ephesians 6:1–3 says, "Children, obey your parents in the Lord, for this is right. Honor your father and mother" (this is the first commandment with a promise), "that it may go well with you and that you may live long in the land." Whether your parents are alive or deceased, you always should show honor that would make them proud. Remember, mixing sin and excuses with God's law is a disgrace to our Father in heaven.

THE SIXTH OF THE TEN COMMANDMENTS

"You shall not murder." This commandment is at the forefront of the abortion controversy these days. I'm really dismayed how our leaders pick and choose what fits their agendas, I like to remind them that God left Ten Commandments, not one, so how can anyone in this world decide someone's fate if they don't follow all the laws of God? Children's lives are taken daily, some before birth and some after. Does either one make it right? According to John 3:17, God did not send His Son into the world to judge but to save the world through Him. So what gives any man or woman the right to pass judgment on anyone when we all sin daily? When we stay in tune with the word of God by loving one another and living with His righteousness, the evil that causes murder will abandon our hearts. We will all have our day in court before the almighty God. I urge all my brothers and sisters to repent of their sins, both known and unknown, and ask God if you can settle your case out of court before Him now.

THE SEVENTH OF THE TEN COMMANDMENTS

"You shall not commit adultery." You could write a book on this one. We think adultery is just having sex outside of marriage, but it's much more than that. Here are three that pop into my mind: (1) Emotional adultery is a feeling of being quickly excited and is openly displayed. (2) Visual adultery is self-explanatory; it is looking at someone with lustful thoughts or staring at someone or his or her body because it is sexually appealing to you. (3) Physical adultery involves bodily contact or activity and voluntary sexual relations between a married individual and someone other than the individual's spouse. Proverbs 6:32 says, "But a man who commits adultery has no sense; whoever does so destroys himself." A man may think he is smart, but after the word of God reaches his heart, only then will he understand that he is just a mere man.

THE EIGHTH OF THE TEN COMMANDMENTS

"You shall not steal." The definition of steal is to take another person's property without permission or legal right and without intending to return it. The Bible describes many forms of stealing we must avoid, and the worst is to take from God. It is to our benefit to remember that God is the source of every good gift that we have. I will name a few instances when some Christians may have stolen something without realizing they had broken this commandment: Has a cashier ever given you too much change, and you did not return it? Have you taken something from your job and said to yourself, "They won't miss it"? Both are considered stealing. Theft is forbidden by God. Ideally, we should be content with what we have and trust God. Philippians 4:19 says, "And this same God who takes care of me will supply all your needs from his glorious riches, which have been given to us in Christ Jesus."

THE NINTH OF THE TEN COMMANDMENTS

"You shall not bear false witness against your neighbor." We all know that lies harm people. Judgment based on false testimony could destroy the lives of innocent people and disrupt the system of justice, and spreading fake stories is being a companion of the wicked. The Bible calls bearing false witness lying, and it compares an individual who does so to a vicious weapon. A person who bears false witness has an evil heart, and the only cure is found in Ezekiel 36:26, which says, "And I will give you a new heart, and I will put a new spirit in you. I will take out your stony, stubborn heart and give you a tender, responsive heart." If you know someone who has a problem with the truth, calling 911 just won't do; you must call on the name that's above every name, and that would be Jesus. Have Him take the wheel!

The Tenth of the Ten Commandments

"You shall not covet." To covet is to yearn to possess something. How often do you find yourself envious of something someone else has? It is sinful to set our desires on anything that is forbidden; we should banish our cravings for whatever does not belong to us, and envy should be expelled from our heart. Be content with what you have. You will never be happy when you covet, unless you are yearning to follow God's law. Life is not about possessions, so let's not compare what we have to what someone else has. First Timothy 6:10 says, "For the love of money is the root of all evil: which while some coveted after, they have erred from the faith, and pierced themselves through with many sorrows."

SUMMARIZING WHAT I WROTE AND LEARNED ABOUT THE TEN COMMANDMENTS

To my understanding these commandments were written to govern the people of God for their own well-being. Many Christians believe that the law saves us, and some believe we are saved by grace. Nowadays a lot of Christians think that there is no law. Even if the law was laid aside to make room for Jesus, the law still reveals our sins. Keep in mind that there is still law as well as grace, and no one can be saved by the law because no person can keep the law. Back in the beginning, Adam and Eve failed to follow God's instructions, as did the Israelites, and today we follow what is convenient for us even if it is forbidden by God. The commandments were given to show how sinful we are and how much we need God for true salvation. To those who say we don't need God's law because of Christ's sacrifice, then why are we still sinners?

ADDICTION

Addiction is the condition of being dependent on a particular substance, thing, or activity. I've read that positive addiction does not dominate one's life. At some point in our lives, we have all been addicted to something. Now ask yourself, "Do I spend more time with any particular substance, thing, or activity than I do the word of God?" One Corinthians 6:12 says, "'All things are lawful for me,' but not all things are helpful. 'All things are lawful for me,' but I will not be dominated by anything." For help, give your life to Christ because He gave His life for you!

AM I SAVED
BY JUST CHANGING MY OLD HABITS?

Many think that to become saved is to change all their old habits, as I did. We must also seek the word of God and believe that Jesus died for our sins, our Lord and Savior was raised, He is who He says, and He does what He says. When the Lord's people start to realize how their sin makes them unhappy, and they repent, their misdeed will turn to contentment. Let us not continue to wrong one another for this is not God's plan for us, and remember sin is the origin of misery and always will be. When God's holy word is in attendance, it shows us how spiritually divine He is, and how unholy we are. Let's not forget that by being human we are bound to make mistakes, but in all you do, praise the Lord God with all your soul and forget not all His benefits. Amen.

Being in Bad Company

You may hear many Christians say, "God told me to be in their company." Please be sure that it is God and not the evil one, whose job is to trick us into entertaining his followers. Nonbelievers have a way of pressuring us into being selfish and inconsiderate toward others, and if we are not careful, they would have us believe that they alone can save us. If you want to ruin your good morals, follow and trust people who tell false truths. "Tell me who you follow, and I will tell you who you are," says 2 John 1:10–11. If anyone comes to your meeting and does not teach the truth about Christ, don't invite that person into your home or give any kind of encouragement. Anyone who encourages such people becomes a partner in their evil work.

BEING SELF-SATISFIED
WILL STUNT YOUR GROWTH!

People are content with the progress they've made as Christians. Some days we just say, "I'm too tired. I can't battle with this sin thing today. I'm okay; I'm in church on Sunday and Bible study on Wednesday. It's all good. I should be covered for today." Our self-approval is the end of all advancements toward salvation, my brothers and sisters. The evils of this world do not take days off. Our fight against acts of evil is an everyday battle; the smallest amount of sin will do more damage than we could ever imagine. We will never have peace until sin is destroyed! When we become lazy and unwilling to fight, and we start living to please ourselves rather than God, this is when Satan lays hands on us. I was once told there are only two possible ways to live: wisely or foolishly. Every day stay armored up in God's word; take time off for no reason! When you feel that you have no fight left within you, think about things of heaven, not the things of this earth, because God's steadfast love endures forever.

BOAST ONLY IN THE LORD

Oh, how I love God, not only when He blesses me but also when He rectifies me for taking credit for the work He has done through me. I love writing devotions, or some may call them testimonies; however, if I were to take credit for them, it would be considered boasting. James 4:16 says as it is, you boast in your arrogance. All such boasting is evil. Proverbs 27:2 says, "Let another praise you, and not your own mouth; a stranger, and not your own lips." Let him who boasts boast in the Lord! Remember the old saying "If you want to make God laugh, tell him your plan"? I don't recall taking credit for all the mistakes I've made, and I'm quick to forget them. Amen. To God, I give all the glory!

Can't Sleep

Have you ever had nights when sleep just won't come, and you just can't figure out why? More than likely we are doing things our own way rather than aligning with the will of God. Try meditating on God's word. For millions of times, if the blessing hadn't already been bestowed on me, I wouldn't be here today, and if you know me, you know this is true. Don't lose sleep trying to handle things your way; rest in the arms of God, and he will bring peace to your nights and days. In God I trust!

STILL A CHILD OF GOD!

When a Christian sins, he or she does not cease to be a Christian, thanks to God! His fellowship is broken, but the person is still God's child. Once we confess our sins and show repentance, God will forgive our sins, and if we truly love God, we will be more fearful of sinning again. Our confession isn't meant to make God know our sins but to make us understand them. The Lord weeps over us and waits to forgive us when we return to Him to restore our fellowship. What a loving God we serve!

CHERRY-PICKING TRESPASSES OF OTHERS IS NOT WISE!

Do you find yourself cherry-picking when it comes to sins? If so, maybe you are looked at as a hypocrite. A misdeed is a sin; it doesn't matter what shape, form, or size it comes in. How we can talk about the sins of others when the trash at our front door needs sweeping? I think there is not enough praying and too much preaching! Each day should start with a prayer: "Lord, as best as I know how, I will attempt to serve as Christ did, and please help me not to judge others when I'm in need of prayer." Amen.

Christian Gentleness

The gentle person attracts the trust of others because in God's sight a kind heart is precious. Be careful not to be so strongly opinionated that others are afraid to express their feelings in your presence. Most importantly, do not criticize or gossip about the brother or sister who falls into sin. You who are godly should gently and humbly help that person back onto the right path—and be careful not to fall into the same temptation yourself (Galatians 6:1). Some people will equate your gentleness with weakness. Not to worry, God loves a gentle heart. God hears a sinner's prayers!

Don't Be Dismayed!

Conflicts and unwanted circumstances will always be a part of this world, but a believer's worst is better than an unbeliever's best. So don't get dismayed when you see the sinful with plenty of material things of this world. It will be good for you to stay humbled with what you have, and not covet the wealth of others. A single day in your court is better than a thousand anywhere else! I would rather be a gatekeeper in the house of my God than live the good life in the homes of the wicked (Psalms 84:10). Our God will withhold no good from those who do what is right. Amen.

COUNT YOUR BLESSINGS

Do you ever take time to reflect on any one day in order to document the many blessings that God has given you? Most of us are worried about things of this world instead of counting our blessings. If we walk around complaining, with our heads down, we can't see the blessings ahead of us. Colossians 3:2 says to set your mind on the things of heaven, not the things on earth. God's word has provided us with tremendous benefits, so let's keep our heads to the sky and give Him all the glory. Amen!

HANDLE YOUR CASES OUT OF COURT!

The Father and the Son and the Holy Spirit are the only judge and jury that I would like to hear my case, for God is the only one who can pardon us. Isaiah 55:7 says, "Let the wicked forsake his way, and the unrighteous man his thoughts; let him return to the Lord, that he may have compassion on him, and our God, for he will abundantly pardon." In the world courts, one can hide and lie, but with God, there is no hiding place. I pray that all my brothers and sisters will work on settling their cases out of court by acknowledging that Jesus is our savior and confessing all known and unknown sins before God. In Jesus's name, amen!

CRAVING

If you or someone you know has had a drug, alcohol, gambling, over-eating, or lying problem, you must know that you cannot love this world or the things it offers you. With each one of these problems, once you start you will continue to crave for more. How much better would your life be if you could flip your world craving to craving the word of God? Anyone who does what pleases God will have eternal life!

1 John 2:15–17

THE CURSED ARE THOSE WHO REFUSE TO REPENT THEIR SINS!

Some people have wondered for years when an unforeseen incident occurs if this is a generational curse. Many have read Exodus 20:5, but please continue to 20:6 to get the full story. There is a trend in the world to blame all wrongdoing on some generational cycle. One thing is for sure: if parents live their life mocking God by being hypocritical, drunken, or anything else that is not in line with the word of God, more than likely the children will follow their lead. God promised that He would show love to those who love and keep His commandments. If we follow His instructions, there is no need to be worried about any curse from your generation. Let's change all our sinful habits and attitudes because what we sow, we will reap. Each is responsible for his or her wrongdoing, so make that change!

Divided We Fall

Most of us call ourselves followers of Christ our Lord, but are we followers when it is convenient for us to be noticed and when we think everyone is looking? God knows each and every heart, and He sees all of those who cause division and false teaching among His people. We should avoid listening to or watching anyone who sows division and pray to God that we don't fall into the trap of the evils put out in the world. Romans 16:17 says, "I appeal to you, brothers [and sisters] to watch out for those who cause divisions and create obstacles contrary to the doctrine that you have been taught; avoid them." Our God is not a God of division but of unity!

AVOID DISUNITY!

I was asked what I think of the world today, and the first thing to come to my mind was division. Some say that division is a part of life. There can be good divisions, which in some cases are necessary, but disunity and division among the people of God is a tragedy that we must do all we can to avoid. Watch out for people who cause division and upset people's faith by teaching things contrary to what we are taught from the word of God. Stay away from them. Such people are not serving Christ our Lord; they are serving their own personal interests. Using smooth talk and glowing words, they deceive innocent people. God is trying to tell us something!

Wish I Could Take It Back

During your struggles, have you ever spontaneously acted or spoken in a way that was not godly, and you can't take back what you've said or done? This is Satan rushing us to destruction. This is what happens when we take matters into our own hands without consulting God. Without the Lord ordering our steps, we soon forget what we have learned and start to depart from his ways. Now we feel that we are lost and out on an island alone. Not to worry. In Matthew, Jesus said, "Rejoice with me, for I have found my sheep which was lost! I tell you that in the same way, there will be more joy in heaven over one sinner who repents than over ninety-nine righteous persons who need no repentance." Our patience is required for God's promise to work in our lives. Thank God for Jesus!

FALSE TEACHING

Titus 1:11says, "They must be silenced, because they are turning whole families away from the truth by their false teaching. And they do it only for money." Young and matured Christians must be aware of false prophets; don't let fast talk and swagger lead you away from the real word of God. One may ask, "How will I know if the actual teaching is from God?" The main question is where the message comes from. If it's not from scripture, you will know it is not from God. False teachings will always tell people what they want to hear or what is appealing to the flesh. They promise much and produce little, and their message is a product of their own; it's not from God. God has placed people around me who know scripture well, and if He did this for me, He would do it for you. Ask and you will receive. All glory to God!

We should not live under the power of fear—fear of holding on to our income, family, friends, and worldly possessions. If we love God, we should live in, on, and under His word and His word only. "God has not given us a spirit of fear and timidity, but of power, love, and self-discipline" (2 Timothy 1:7). When our time expires from this world, we have to go by ourselves. Like the old gospel song, send me and I'll go!

Faithfulness

Encouragement

Abundance

Redeemed

Seek God in all your times of anxiety!

FORGIVENESS

Do you ever think about all the times you have been forgiven? If so, it shouldn't be hard to forgive those who have sinned against you. At times, pains of the past come back when you remember someone who caused you distress. This lets you know that you're still holding on to your past, which makes it hard to forgive. This is no way for a God-fearing person to live. Always remember: when you ask God to forgive your sins as you forgive those who have sinned against you, this is key for forgiveness, and Jesus shows us how it's done (Luke 23:34). Your past is gone because anyone who belongs to Christ has become a new person. The old life is gone; a new life has begun! Amen.

GIVE MORE THANKS!

We have all been guilty, as well as ignorant, for not giving God thanks for all things, not just at mealtime. We have made it routine at meal-time to bow our heads and give thanks for the food we receive. Is it a heartfelt thanks or just habit? God deserves our thanks all day, every day—when we wake up each day or when we look at the car(s) in our driveway He deserves our thanks for our children and grandchildren, our home and what's in it, our job, the air we breathe, and so much more. I will thank you, Lord, with my whole heart; I will tell of all the marvelous things You have done (Psalms 9:1).

GOD IS ETERNAL

In the last thirty days, there have been four places of worship destroyed, some accidental and some purposely because of hate. Let's put things in perspective. Anything made by human hands is temporary, but what God does is eternal. These days the emphasis is more about man-made objects than winning souls back to God. Luke 12:34 says, "For where your treasure is, there will your heart be also." Every individual has a role to play in helping someone get back to God, but first we must see the sin that is in us and stop worrying about the sins of others; then we are on our way to salvation. Is there any good in filling the pews with thousands when no souls have been won back to God? The time is now for us to put our trust in the one and only eternal God from this point forward! Amen.

GOD KNOWS YESTERDAY, TODAY, AND TOMORROW

The more I read God's word, the more I see how it relates to what is going on in the world today. In Exodus 7, God said to Moses, "You shall speak all that I command you," and your brother Aaron shall tell Pharaoh, the king of Egypt, to let the people of Israel go. With all the disasters and plagues, He refuses to listen to our government today. Like Pharaoh, our government feared that people different from them were becoming too many and too mighty, and both of them said let's deal with these people harshly and slow any plans that they may have. We can't continue thinking our wrongs are hidden from God because He created all and knows all. So it doesn't matter what position or knowledge we may hold in this world; there are two choices we have to deal with in our present situation: God's way or Pharaoh's way. The moral of this story is to do to others as you would have them do!

Fix Your Mind on His Word!

Have you ever found yourself walking through the church doors with your mind on things of this world? When this happens, your focus is not fixed on hearing the word of God. As soon as you take your seat, your mind starts to wander everywhere, i.e., "The game starts at one o'clock; I hope the service is done before it starts" or "What will I have to eat after the service?" or "Why did Sister wear that outfit?" or "Look at the brother over there falling asleep." If your mind is focused on these things, your heart will follow. Before you enter the church doors, ask God to remove everything not relating to His word and to fix your heart and mind on Him, and Him alone. Ephesians 5:25–26 says, "Christ loved the church. He gave up his life for her to make her holy and clean, washed by the cleansing of God's word." God will fix it!

I always thought that God's greatest miracles were when He healed my sick and aching body or provided for me financially. As I look back on my life, I can see that the greatest miracles occurred when God gave me the breakthrough from the strongholds and my destructive behaviors. I now understand that I am a living testimony to God's greatness, and if you know me, you know these words are real. Stop for a minute and take a look back at your life, and praise God for being here today. Glory to God!

I'm God's Property!

Are you being haunted by negative thoughts from your past that pop up when something you hear or see triggers these memories? This is the evil one at work, doing his best to shake your spirit and place doubt in your mind. Remember, you have been made new by the Creator, so don't be afraid to speak out loud to the evil one, saying, "I'm God's property!" Brothers and sisters, I don't consider that I have made it on my own. But one thing I do is forget what lies behind and look forward to what lies ahead. I press on to reach the goal for the heavenly prize for which God, through Christ Jesus, is calling us (Philippians 3:13–14). Amen!

God's Word!

I am blessed to have family members and friends who have been called to teach and preach the word of God. They help me in so many ways and show me that each one of us has a gift that can be used to lift up someone in need of prayer. I'm not attempting to preach; I'm seeking to be taught when the time comes that I am called to share what I have learned. I will be ready and willing to speak God's word, not my own. "As for me, I am in your hands—do with me as you think best" (Jeremiah 26:14). Amen!

GOOD SHEPHERD

We are people who often go astray in our hearts; this is unintentional and caused by the temptations of this world. The good news is the Good Shepherd will leave the flock to search for the one lost sheep. It is impossible to do anything to resist the evils of this world without the Good Shepherd. He needs to order our step daily to avoid the enticement to go astray. We should be enchanted with the word of God, even when it rebukes us. This is proof we are benefiting from it. The word of God creates and sustains life. Jesus said, "I am the Good Shepherd. The good shepherd sacrifices his life for the sheep" (John 10:11). Amen!

Habit

If you are having problems understanding the things of God and don't understand why you do the things you do, it's time to take a self-inventory and ask God to send his Holy Spirit to give you spiritual direction. Don't allow any habits to lead you to sin. As you know, a repeated action becomes a habit, so repeat God's word every day, and it will become a habit to help you resolve all that you don't understand. The good news is when you trust in God's word, He will open doors of opportunity for you. Trust in His holy word!

Have Faith and Believe!

As the year draws to a close and we start to make our resolutions, I would like us to lay down our requests at the cross and by faith walk away, believing that it is done. Let no doubt enter your heart and mind. Remember in John, chapter 4, when the government official's son was near death, and he heard that Jesus had come to Galilee. He went to Jesus pleading for Him to go to his home and heal his son who was about to die. Jesus told the official to go back home. "Your son will live!" The official believed what Jesus said and went home. When he arrived, his son had recovered. Once we lay it down and stay out of the way, let God and let go. Only then can we have the same results as the official. I paraphrased in some areas to get the full picture but read the entire chapter of John 4. This New Year let's fertilize our lives with scripture by meditating on the word of God daily. Happy New Year!

Does God really care if we sin? Yes, He does! This is a question the devil wants us to keep asking until we think that it's okay to continue to sin. Being a Christian is not a one-time stamp of approval where God no longer cares how we live. Hebrews 4:15 says, "This High Priest of ours understands our weaknesses, for he faced all of the same testing we do, yet he did not sin." We cannot or will not keep our devotion to God perfectly clean, but it should at least be our aim. Don't be fooled by anyone; God has no sin, so do you think He doesn't care about the rest of His children when He sent His sin-free son to die for our sins? We must keep teaching the word of God to ourselves daily.

HEARTS AND MINDS

Some people can quote scripture easily and remember where to find it; some people take scripture to heart and try their best to live by it. Remember, Satan believes the truth about God in his mind, but he does not live for God. He does not trust God. The heart and thoughts are both needed for us to truly fellowship with and trust God. One of the most significant shortfalls of this age is that the head counts more than the heart, and people are far readier to learn than to love, instead of bringing the heart and mind together. Ask the Holy Spirit to program your heart and brain to work as one to trust and believe in the word of God, in Jesus's name!

Put Your Trust in His Holy Word

History shows us that many people are taken from us for trying to make this world a better place to live. They were prevented by death or captivity from continuing to make changes. We know that the evil one is still at work, trying to separate us from the love of God, but all who trust in Jesus have the comfort of knowing that not even death can separate us from His love. He is always ready to protect us, and His love endures forever! Two Timothy 4:2 tells us, "Preach the word of God. Be prepared, whether the time is favorable or not. Patiently correct, rebuke, and encourage your people with good teaching." Pray to our Lord and Savior to help us identify all barriers that the ungodly erect to keep us from His love. Amen!

His Will

Many are called to spread God's good news by writing or speaking. I enjoy a good sermon as well as a good book, especially when they relate to the word of God. Once the lecture is over and the book is closed, most of us find our way back to the unfaithful and untrusting world of false bravado. We should use the word of God as much as we watch our favorite TV shows or spend time on social media and any other worldly device that takes us away from time with God. Favor only comes from the will of God; no other activity in this world can give favor as our Lord does. Ephesians 5:15–17 says, "Be very careful, then, how you live—not as unwise but as wise, making the most of every opportunity" in these evil days. "Therefore do not be foolish, but understand what the Lord's will is." Amen!

WHEN AND HOW TO PASS JUDGMENT

Do you ever find yourself judging someone's appearance, choice, competence, or sociability? "Do not judge others, and you will not be judged" (Matthew 7:1). Do you think that judging right and wrong is a bad thing? Jesus suggests that it's not the act of judging but the attitude in which we make judgments. There may be times when it is necessary for you to form an opinion or conclusion about someone or something, and the key to this is attitude. We should be civil when it comes to judging because our Lord has been so gracious and generous to us, and we at times are unworthy of His support. Ask God to send his Holy Spirit to empty out and cleanse your heart of any negativity before judging. Amen.

I Believe

When we become born-again Christians, we are asked, "Do you believe?" At the moment we would answer yes. To me, the next question should be "Are you ready to confess all known and unknown sins before God?" At the time of this life-changing event, our own sins are in question—not to worry about anybody or anything else. Just consider yourself before God, who knows all and is all. We can't deal with our sins until we see them as God does. One John 1:9 says, "If we confess our sins, He is faithful and righteous to forgive us our sins and cleanse us from all unrighteousness." And remember, Jesus promised to make us free when releasing our sins to Him. If we believe in Christ, the impossible becomes possible!

I Know He Watches Over Me

I sent out a heartfelt devotion a few weeks back, and an old friend asked if I was okay or if I was sick. This stayed with me for a while, so I went into prayer with God and asked Him why this was laying so heavy on my heart. After a few moments of silence, I burst out in laughter, thinking if only my friend had seen me before I gave my life over to Christ, he would have really thought I was sick. I do thank my friend for his concern, but above all I give all glory to God that I'm not where I once was. The moral of this story is whatever your life was in the past, God can fix your future. Amen!

He Watches Over Me

I'm sending this to each of you as a thank-you and a testimony. None of you have any idea what I have been going through with my medical bills. It has put a strain on our finances. I prayed and talked with God about my trip to Florida because I almost canceled it. After praying, I laid down all my burdens and let God take the wheel. Then His Holy Spirit told me not to ask anyone for anything, and I followed the instruction I was given. God and each one of you came to my rescue. I am so thankful and blessed for all the gifts and also to have a family like all of you. If I've ever said or done anything to cause you pain, please forgive me. I pray that each of us will do all we can in words and deeds to make our Lord Jesus proud. Thanks to you all for a great birthday!

How Do You Know That You Are Saved?

Romans 10:9–10 says, "If you confess with your mouth that Jesus is Lord and believe in your heart that God raised him from the dead, you will be saved." I wouldn't stop with this scripture. I would tell them, "If you knew me twenty years ago, you would say that I had gone from bad to worse." After I surrendered myself to my Lord and Savior, things shifted from good to best. Being saved doesn't mean you are mistake or sin free; it means you are aware of sin and will repent to God in prayer and with a sincere heart. Remember to forgive those who have sinned against you. Repentance and forgiveness go hand in hand! Amen.

When the word imprisonment comes up, we think it means being be-hind bars, but contrary to this thought, many of us are imprisoned by our flesh daily. There is a war within, and God's Spirit battles with our sinfulness. People who try to live without relying on God's Spirit will wind up being led by the sinfulness of the flesh. Before you go to bed tonight, use God's word as a weapon against any ungodly thoughts, and when morning approaches, your praises to God should be the first thing out of your mouth before the attacks of the flesh begin. Galatians 5:16 says, "So I say, let the Holy Spirit guide your lives. Then you won't be doing what your sinful nature craves." Thanks to the almighty God for never getting tired of blessing us. Amen!

What will we do when we are called to stand in the presence of God? Three things come into my mind: (1) bow down before Him, (2) thank and praise Him for all his blessings, and (3) do not mention any good deeds we've done before Him because for every sound act there are many iniquities. As I meditate on His presence, I realize that He is always with us; it is we who turn from Him to please our flesh. Our sins undermine our mission to experience His presence. We can't be joyful Christians if we don't know that God is present always. Take time to read Psalms 139:7–10. Amen.

In the book of Romans, Paul called on us to offer our bodies as a living sacrifice to God. With this sacrifice we commit to a life of holiness that pleases God. In my opinion, it is very difficult for people in this world to make any commitment to obedience without exception. We are known for saying, "This sin is not so bad" or "This is the last time I'll do this" or "I'll just sneak a peek." Thinking this way erodes our commitment to God and makes the next excuse that much easier. Christ sacrificed for us, and we should do a better job to return the love!

Is It Possible for a Human to Make America or the World Great Again?

First, let's think back to when it was great. Grab your Bible and start at the beginning in the Garden of Eden. It's clear that life in Eden was simple and innocent, with plenty of food and water, no unpleasant experiences, and no pollution or wars. This was before the Fall. After the Fall, sin came into the world through one man. We had a chance to get it right with the instructions God gave us, and from the Fall until now, we missed the first step in making sure that we walked in God's will. There was only one man who walked on this earth who could save us, and his name is Jesus Christ. There is no other person who can make this possible!

There's something about the name Jesus!

Jesus Is Our Ark!

How seriously do we take the wrath of God? In my opinion, God's forgiveness is taken for granted when we speak ungodly and act righteously. We should not just hear the word of God but feed on it 24/7! When I think of God's wrath, Noah's ark always comes to mind. God saw that the earth had become corrupt and was filled with violence, so he had Noah build a giant boat before His wrath hit the planet. We should look to Jesus as our ark, and if we don't get on board, we will find no safety outside the ark and no salvation outside of Jesus. We can all be saved from the corruption of this world by following the commands of God and avoiding sin, so obedience can be perfected. Amen.

Why is it that the law makes no mention of repentance? Is it because our Lord and Savior knew that most humans' repentance was out of fear of punishment and not heartfelt? Sometimes it takes a rooster to crow or an earthquake to open the doors of a prison before a man or woman can have heartfelt repentance. God uses both trials and joys so He can produce a better mind and heart in us sinners toward Him. Let's work at being more Christ-like!

LEAVE ALL YOUR TROUBLES BEHIND

How long will we wrestle with the difficulties of this world? It is pointless to fight these problems on our own; they will reappear again and again. Our struggles keep us consumed with negativity, leaving us little time to spend with our Lord and Savior. Today be still and take all of your worries before God in prayer, and watch Him quiet the storms that trouble you.

To God be all the glory!

LISTEN

I've found that one of our biggest mistakes as young Christians is thinking that we can keep all of God's precepts. We are not perfect as Christ is, but we must work at maintaining the commands God left for us to keep our spiritual strength. If we are faithful in following God's laws as best as we can, He will help us when we fall or are tempted to break His rules. I remember when I couldn't hear or didn't want to listen to the soft voice of God directing me. Now God knows that my heart, mind, and soul are on Him, and I can hear the quiet voice saying what Jesus would do. God speaks to us all. The question is are we listening? Deuteronomy 6:25 (NLT) says, "For we will be counted as righteous when we obey all the commands the Lord our God has given us." Amen!

My daily devotion was about listening. At times I think all of us are quick to speak and slow to hear. If we refuse to listen to wise counseling, we are destined for failure. With that being said, we should discern who we are listening to because some counsel may have good intentions but can lead you astray if they are not following the word of God. Ask God to send His Holy Spirit to help you identify godly counsel. Make your ears attentive to wisdom, and when speaking, be obedient to the word of God. Amen.

LONELINESS

All my life I have been around people. I always had someone close by my side, and still there were times when I felt lonely. We can try to solve our loneliness with people who will satisfy our fixated behavior, but this will not remedy the problem. These are not the people God has placed in our lives; these people are your choices. You can rely upon the people that God places in our lives, and some of us may call them heaven sent. You will know they mean well when they keep it at one hundred (this means keeping it real), even when it hurts to hear the truth. Psalms 25:16–18 says, "Turn to me and have mercy, for I am alone and in deep distress. My problems go from bad to worse. Oh, save me from them all! Feel my pain and see my trouble. Forgive all my sins." Try God, and He will fix it. Consider all the great things He has done for you. Amen!

It's All About Love

In our lives, we have all been hurt by someone we love or care about, and we hold on to that pain until it turns to hate, not realizing that the evil one has planted a seed of malice in our existence. We need to pay forward the same forgiveness that God has given us. "Love marks the children of God, but hate is the sure sign of those who will inherit the wrath of God." Let's not become another Cain, who doesn't confess his sins but only complains about the punishment that comes from his transgressions. All are guilty, regardless of our sins or poor decisions. God's arms are always open, and it is a free gift, not that we deserve it. Amen!

LOVE ONE ANOTHER WHILE WE ARE STILL ALIVE!

I feel we take for granted the time we have left in this life. Have you ever been critical of someone for saying or doing something that you say and do daily? We should be careful about what we think of, say to, and do toward others because there may not be a tomorrow. When death comes, we tend to recollect all the good things about a person, but by that time apologizing and making amends are out of reach. Your good wishes at the funeral are too late for the person to hear. One Corinthians 13:4–7 says, "Love is patient and kind. Love is not jealous or boastful or proud or rude. It does not demand its own way. It is not irritable, and it keeps no record of being wronged. It does not rejoice about injustice but rejoices whenever the truth wins out. Love never gives up, never loses faith, is always hopeful, and endures through every circumstance." Jesus Christ showed love and forgiveness for us; we should pay it forward while there is still time.

More Like Christ

When we accept Christ as Lord and Savior, some might think this will stop them from sinning. This couldn't be further from the truth. We can't act or be like other people and claim we have accepted Christ as Savior. This makes us hypocrites. We can't have it both ways. Jesus calls us to witness, not to judge! Let's stop with the paybacks and take all our concerns to the cross. Remember, Jesus said, "Father, forgive them, for they do not know what they are doing." Matthew 5:44–45 says, "But I say, love your enemies! Pray for those who persecute you! In this way, you will be acting as true children of your Father in heaven. For he gives his sunlight to both the evil and the good, and sends rain on the just and the unjust alike." For this season and every day let's be more like Christ. Amen!

I have publicly identified with the greatest act of human history: the death, burial, and resurrection of Jesus Christ. This baptism was my personal testimony to my passage from the old life to my new life in Christ Jesus. I have joined the ranks of all the believers in Christ Jesus. I thank God for all he has done for me and also thank the three men of God—Bishop Johnny Jenkins, Pastor Billy Oliver, and my brother Malcolm Hawkins—who witnessed this wonderful event on Sunday, June 3, 2018. In closing, if you have tried everything and still feel you are falling short, try God!

My Thoughts

I am in the young stage of regeneration, and I'm reading more and listening to what's going on around me. I heard an Evangelical leader say that God put Donald Trump in office to save this country. I agree that He put him in office, but only Jesus can save. What I'm about to say are my thoughts and mine alone. It's time that we stop building up and trusting a man or woman more than God because sooner or later that person will let you down. There is so much hatred and fear among people today, and this is why I think Mr. Trump was placed in office: to show us that God is not pleased with us. Now that we are separated by color, gender, and political parties, I think we'd better start changing. The way things are now makes me think of Genesis 11:1–9, when God came down and looked at what was going on and was not pleased. To me, this country should be called the Place of Babel because no one understands what the other is saying. God made people speak many different languages so they couldn't work together. What's so sad about people today is that we speak the same language but still don't understand one another. Fear not because we have Psalms 30:5 that says, "For his anger lasts only a moment, but his favor lasts a lifetime! Weeping may endure through the night, but joy comes with the morning."

NEGATIVITY

When trials and tribulations come into the lives of humans, the first thing that happens is the mind shifts to the negative mode, i.e., what's going to happen next, why me, what have I done to deserve this, and so on. If you put your trust in God, He will turn bad things into favor. Don't give your mind a chance to shift. Start praying and asking God to provide you with direction. Negativity is like a wildfire: the more fuel you give it, the faster it will spread. God blesses those who patiently endure testing and temptation. Afterward, they will receive the crown of life that God promised to those who love Him (James 1:12). So let's stop the negative thinking; instead give praise to your Lord and Savior for always giving you His very best. Amen.

No Shame

If you are in the company of people who make you feel ashamed to speak God's truth, you are in bad company, for there is no reason you should ever feel this way. God's word is holy. Let no one or nothing make you feel shame when you speak God's word because embarrassment is not for the holy. There is nothing in holiness to be embarrassed about. "But it is no shame to suffer for being a Christian. Praise God for the privilege of being called by his name!" (1 Peter 4:16). For great is the Lord and greatly to be praised!

No temptation has overtaken you that is not common among humans. God is faithful, and He will not let you be tempted beyond your ability, but with the temptation He will provide the way to escape so you may be able to endure it. Put on the whole armor of God so you are able to stand against the schemes of the devil. Satan's thoughts can tempt us, but as long as these thoughts or feelings are rejected, sin has not been committed. However, if the thoughts or feelings are accepted and acted upon, mentally or openly, God's will is not obeyed, and sin is committed. Let no one say when he or she is tempted, "I am being tempted by God," for God cannot be tempted with evil, and He tempts no one. Individuals are tempted when they are lured and enticed by their own desire. When desire has been conceived, it gives birth to sin, and when sin is fully grown, it brings forth death. Keep the armor of God on at all times, and pray without ceasing.

With all of the natural disasters in the world, many lives and homes are taken from us, and our faith is nonexistent. The only way to restore our confidence is to spend more time in God's word. Our faith must be like the tree planted by the water, and thy shall not be moved. For us to have faith like this, we need to become a new creation that only our Creator can grant. What this world may tear down, our God will build up. For we know that when this earthly tent we live in is destroyed, we will have a house in heaven, an eternal body made for us by God and not by human hands (2 Corinthians 5:1). Amen!

OH, GIVE ME SAMUEL'S EAR

I started writing when I heard someone say to focus on the cross and not on what we don't have. When we realize how much Christ suffered, our complaints should be silenced. Sunday morning sermons are not just for showing up and shouting amen. We should listen with Samuel's ear and then go out and share the word of God and your blessings with others. Each one of us has someone in our lives who is hurting. A Christian's job is not to keep quiet and stay away; it is to share the glory of God's blessings. Our true spirit as Christians should be one of love and sympathy. Let your love be real not only in words but also in deeds and in truth. When you have the chance, look up the poem "The Child Samuel," by James D. Burns, and pray each day for God to give you Samuel's ear. Amen.

Our Actions Show Who We Follow

We don't have to broadcast that we are Christians or always want the best seat up front to get noticed. Our efforts should show who we are, and by believing that Christ died for us, we should conduct ourselves as believers in Christ Jesus. If the Lord came to you today and asked, "Are you a faithful follower of mine?" can you answer yes without hesitating? Most of us would say, "I sin occasionally, but yes, Lord, I am a follower." The Lord knows all too well all that is done. The first words out of our mouth should be "Yes, Lord! As bad as I am, I believe You, and You alone can save me because Your precious blood can cleanse me from all my sins." Amen!

OUR WOUNDS TURN TO SINS

I gave my honest opinion to someone, and when that person came back to me, I learned that my opinion hadn't helped the situation. In reply, I said that I hated to hear that. "I don't have all the answers, but I can direct you to somebody who can make the impossible possible, and that would be our Father in heaven." Sometimes we carry our wounds from childhood until they turn into sin and self-pity, which leads to depending on this world's substances for healing, and when self-pity starts, we go from bad to worse. One Corinthians 13:11 says, "When I was a child, I spoke and thought and reasoned like a child. But when I grew up, I put away childish things." Whatever wounds you are carrying can't compare to the wounds of our Lord and Savior. If you don't have a Bible, use your phone, tablet, or computer when your past starts influencing you. Read Isaiah 53:5, and compare your scars to what Jesus suffered for you! Lay down all of your hurt before God because He is always ready to save the unsaved. Amen.

When I was a young sinner, Satan kept me afraid of turning my life over to Christ. Fear of my sins overshadowed all that God had promised. We can no longer afford to let fear keep us from our wise, loving, and sovereign God. Our job as Christians is to show that the fear of their sins is not higher than the love of God. His love is higher than the earth to the heavens. When fear hits, go to Genesis 50:20: "You intended to harm me, but God intended it all for good. He brought me to this position so I could save the lives of many people." All I can say is God kept me!

People are afraid of the direction in which our leaders are going. Think about Romans 13:1: "Let everyone be subject to the governing authorities…" The way things are in this world makes me wonder if God instituted all people in power. I know that we should show respect to governing bodies, but we should not compromise our beliefs or act in an evil manner that dishonors God. Exodus 9:12 says, "But the Lord hardened Pharaoh's heart, and he would not listen to Moses and Aaron…" To me, this is what's happening now. If our leaders heard, read, studied, memorized, and meditated on God's word, we could follow them free of worries. Amen!

Person, Place, or Thing

Most of us at some point in our lives have felt as if we had been consumed and almost destroyed by addictions, family, relationships, or employment. Do you remember being taught at an early age about nouns, i.e. person, place, or thing? Any one of the three can separate us from the word of God. The purpose is for this wicked world to make you think that you can't survive without these nouns, and once you start thinking this way, you will turn into a victim because you have been overwhelmed. Stop thinking that you have to have any of these things when God has his angels ready to lead you and keep you safe. Hebrews 12:7 says, "Endure hardship as discipline; God is treating you as his children. For what children are not disciplined by their father?" God's love is sufficient!

PRAYER CHANGES THINGS!

What a wonderful world this would be if only we would stop judging and criticizing one another and start praying for each other. Judging is considered a sin in the eyes of our Lord and Savior. My brothers and sisters, God does not tolerate attacks on His people, and when you cause pain to others, you also cause sadness in God. Ephesians 4:31–32 says, "Let all bitterness and wrath and anger and clamor and slander be put away from you, along with all malice. Be kind to one another, tenderhearted, forgiving each other, just as God in Christ also has forgiven you." How long will we continue asking for God's grace while making little to no effort to stop our sinful way of living? And when will we stop mistaking God's generosity with his anger? Amen!

Preacher Charles Spurgeon said, Let all of us make great effort to support the prayerfulness of the church because if that becomes weak, everything becomes weak. Therefore, lift your drooping hands and strengthen your weak knees. Spiritual evil can only be conquered by a life of prayer. When we fail to pray, the enemy easily defeats us.

Can you imagine having to travel fifty or sixty miles with your children to get a shower once a week? Four years have passed since contaminated water in Flint, Michigan, has troubled the people in this city, including children, with memory loss, body rashes, and other illnesses. I'm asking everyone to step outside their haven and, for just a moment, send prayers to the people of Flint. The church you attend is only one part of the body; when other parts of the body experience pain, the entire body is affected, and we are all one body with many members. Jesus's power and compassion reached all people; He came to save everyone.

What would have happened if Jesus only saved the Jewish people? We would all be in trouble. We know that prayer changes things, so let's get at it and send those prayers out to Flint. Amen!

Have you ever awakened with the pressures of this world weighing down on your heart and mind, and you're looking for someone or something to lash out at? I found a couple of reasons why this happens, and there are many more. When we take off our armor or lay it down for a moment, this opens the door for the evil one to attack, and when we retire for the night, our last conversation and thoughts should be with God, thanking Him for taking us through the day and preparing us for what's to come. Stay alert! Watch out for your great enemy, the devil. He prowls around like a roaring lion, looking for someone to devour (1 Peter 5:8). Remember, apart from God we can do nothing! There is no greater love than the love God has for us. Amen.

QUIET TIME

When it's time to be quiet before God so He can speak to us and teach us, our conscience will bring to mind something that might set us apart from Christ. Whatever you do, don't try to store your sin away; plead guilty, and repent before God. Ask God to send his Holy Spirit to walk with you daily, so when your mind brings up any sin old or new, you can quickly turn it over before God. This is a daily fight, so stay armored up for battle. "If we confess our sins, he is faithful and just to forgive us our sins and to cleanse us from all unrighteousness" (1 John 1:9). Amen.

RELIGIONS

Why are there different religions, and is there one right religion? Different religions are based on different responses that people have to God's word. True religion teaches the truth that is based on the Bible, not on human philosophies, and true religion will help you to know God. Jesus said you shall love the Lord your God with all your heart, soul, and mind, and you will also love your neighbor as yourself. Whatever group or church you attend, make sure it teaches scripture as it is written, and let no one pick apart scripture to fit his or her needs. Before reading any scripture, ask God for insight to open your heart and mind to what you are about to read. You should ponder God's word deeply, analyzing and meditating on it. Then do all you can that you might not sin against thee. One love under God!

Repent

We can't repent perfectly any more than we can live perfectly. To repent is to change your mind about sin and Christ, and all the countless things about God. Repentance won't make you see Christ, but seeing Christ will give you repentance. Words from Charles Spurgeon. When we repent, is it to make an excuse for the sin we've committed or is it to lead you to the fullness of life with Jesus? I'm hoping it's the latter of the two.

To God be all the honor and glory!

RESOLUTIONS

It's that time of the year when we start thinking about resolutions for the New Year. When I asked God why I fall short on my decisions, God's Holy Spirit didn't take long to answer my question. It's probably you! If you are trying to stop a particular substance, thing, or activity, or if you are trying to start any of the three, you cannot change it on your own. When we try to do it ourselves, this is where we fall short. We need God's Holy Spirit to order our steps daily. If we say that Jesus can save us, why do we always interfere with Him while He is transforming us into a new life? This year, make your resolution to do God's will, and your ability to change will come easier. "It is no longer I who live, but Christ lives in me…" (Galatians 2:20).

When you fight dark with more darkness, all you get is devilry. Don't seek your own resolution without consulting with the almighty God, who will shine His light of truth on your situation. Two wrongs have never made anything right. The evils of this world would love to see us killing, stealing, and destroying one another, so let's be reserved when it comes to retaliation on anyone. We should ask God to teach us how to live and to lead us along the right path. Dear friends, never take revenge. Leave that to the righteous anger of God. "For the scriptures say, 'I will take revenge; I will pay them back,' says the Lord" (Romans 12:19).

SACRIFICE

I was sent a message about the dangers of human virtues, and one read "religion without sacrifice." I asked myself, "If God were to ask me to stop gossiping, lying, complaining, judging others, eating or drinking too much, or spitting out words before I taste them, could I or would I make the sacrifice to stop?" These are small requests compared to what Abraham was willed to sacrifice (Genesis 22:1–10). And then there was the sacrifice of sacrifices by our Lord Jesus Christ (Philippians 2:6–8). When God asks anything of us, no matter how difficult it is, do it. He will bless you in ways that will both surprise and delight you. Amen.

I've been a Golden State Warriors fan since the early 1970s when they were headed to Houston for game seven. I felt bad thinking about all they had to go through to get to that point. This was heartfelt. Then the guilt set in because not once in my life had I ever felt this way about the pain Christ suffered for me on the cross. This is shameful. Lord, please send your Holy Spirit to me to put Christ above any and everything in my life. In Jesus's name!

As humans in this world, we can never be totally free of sin. Our only way to fight and escape the temptation of sin is to pray to God that He will fill us with His Holy Spirit so we may have the strength not only to deny but also to overcome the sins of this world. I think all Christians know our Lord and Savior was raised from His death after His sacrifice for our sins. This does not give us the right to continue to let our rebellious hearts lead us away from God. Repentance is beautiful. Just think if we consulted with God before making decisions on everyday issues; each day would be brighter than the next. Remember 1 John 1:10: "If we claim we have not sinned, we are calling God a liar and showing that his word has no place in our hearts." Keep praying. God does hear a sinner's prayer!

Have you ever found yourself in a position where you know it's time to speak up to someone, but you don't want to hurt their feelings or start a conflict? As believers, we may find ourselves in many difficult situations, but as Christ told Paul in a vision, "Don't be afraid! Speak out!...For I am with you" (Acts 18:9–10). We can't forget that we are Christ's messengers to those who are in need of help, and we can't be spineless and not speak up due to fear. We will do more harm than good. The choice is to cause a minute of discomfort or a lifetime of pain. Remember to do this gently and respectfully. Always ask God to send His Holy Spirit when you find it difficult to speak up. This will keep your conscience clear. Amen!

People who support Christ and those who support their flesh will both have storms befall them. I'm sure each of us has faced both sides at one point or another. When you follow the flesh, you side with it; when you follow Christ, you side with Christ. The world dominates a nonbeliever's life, and we all know what that leads to, while God governs the believer, which leads to eternal life. If your life forecasts storms ahead, go to the Lord and ask Him to fix it before the storm hits, then let His will work, not yours. When God is at work in your life, He will bring never-ending change! Amen.

Some people you listen to will make submitting to God's will difficult, and some will make it easy if they are speaking from God's word. Before I started to listen for His voice and meditate on His word, I found myself submitting to things of this world. When we fail to submit to the will of God, we will always suffer the consequences. After offering my life to Christ, the storms still came, but who better than God would you prefer to ride out a storm with! (James 4:7–10)

Temptation is defined as a desire to do something, especially something wrong or unwise. Did you know it is our desires that will lure us in and, if acted on, will cause us to sin? When temptation and sin get together, they give birth to rebellion. From there the truth is hidden from those around us, but there is no hiding from God. When enticed to do things outside of God's will, be quick to tell Jesus to take the wheel because the more contemplating you do about temptation, the sooner it will become action. The impulse will come to us, so we must stay armored up in God's word. Matthew 6:13 says, "And lead us not into temptation, but deliver us from the evil one." And Psalms 101:3 states, "I will not look with approval on anything that is vile. I hate what faithless people do; I will have no part in it." Keep these two scriptures with you at all times, and be prepared to use them. All glory to God!

Have you ever read Paul's testimony in Acts 26? What an example he is for Christians to follow when giving a statement about God. Testimonies I've heard always start by giving honor to God, and then it becomes all about oneself. We often dramatize our testimony evidence and use it to bring attention to ourselves, but we should use it to show how God has spiritually awakened us and protected us, which demonstrates how great God is. We have all had an opportunity to show how life is when we are running something, so let's take the back seat and give God the control. "Whatever you do, do it all for the glory of God" (1 Corinthians 10:31). Amen!

THE FORGIVENESS OF GOD

We all know that we serve a forgiving God, so how long will we continue to sin, acknowledging that it is okay, I'll be forgiven? The sad thing is most of us have become oblivious to our iniquities. This happens so much that we have become a world full of careless people. We have become the spitting image of the Israelites who, after all the blessings they received, continued doing what brought them pleasure, disregarding the commandments of God. This is why we should pay close attention to our conduct toward God and each other. If we are judging or hurting people, we are better off not talking, and if we must speak, we should taste our words before spitting them out. Proverbs 3:5–7 says to trust in the Lord with all your heart; do not depend on your own understanding. Seek his will in all you do, and he will show you which path to take. Don't be impressed with your own wisdom. Instead, fear the Lord and turn away from evil. Then you will find favor with both God and people!

The Routes Don't Matter

Some of us took a long way around to come to Christ, and I do mean the long, hard road. For some, however, the route was untroubled. For the ones who chose the rough way around, do not blame or hate the ones who came to Christ much sooner without all of the obstacles. Jesus Christ came into the world to save sinners, and no matter which route you take or how many times you fall, get up and repent and begin again. "It's not how you come to Christ; it's that you come to Him." One Peter 1:6 says, "So be truly glad. There is wonderful joy ahead, even though you must endure many trials for a little while." We can cast all our anxieties on the Lord because he cares for us. Amen!

THE SPECK IN MY EYE

How many of us are still doing and saying things we did decades ago? Have you surrendered all of these things over to God, or are you still trying to handle them yourself? It would be best to use all our effort to glorify the name of Jesus while confessing our own unworthiness in prayer. If we refuse to take up the cross and turn over all of our unrighteousness to God, growing old will seem like a misfortune rather than a blessing. "How can you think of saying to your friend, 'Let me help you get rid of that speck in your eye,' when you can't see past the log in your own eye? Hypocrite! First get rid of the log in your own eye; then you will see well enough to deal with the speck in your friend's eye" (Matthew 7:4–5). Amen!

As a teenager and young adult, I chose to party, drink, and whatever else went along with that type of living. I paid no attention to the voice telling me this was not the way, thinking that the voice I was hearing wanted to spoil my fun. Now I know it was the voice of God's Holy Spirit, not preventing me from enjoying life but saving me from total disaster. Listening to instructions is one thing, and heeding them is another. Think about Adam, who heard God's voice but, like me, felt the spoken voice was stopping him from having fun. As Christians we must let young people know that the voice telling you not to sin is a friend, not a foe; the choice is yours to listen to the flesh or to God's voice, which has no sin. God's way is the only way!

THEY ARE IN A BETTER PLACE!

What a start to the New Year: there have been six deaths among family and friends. Sorrow never had a chance to pass before hearing about the next departure. Condolences are kind, but they don't give much comfort as we deal with the loss of loved ones. We can always find support in God's word as I did in John 14:2–3, when Jesus said, "I am going to prepare a place for you. When everything is ready, I will come and get you, so that you will always be with me where I am." What a comfort to know that my family and friends who have passed on are now with Jesus in the place he prepared for them. Those of us who are left here must take God's word and apply it to our lives daily, and not let our amnesia of God's mercy be the cause of our present misery. Amen.

Do we love the things of this world more than we love God? As we all know, where the love is, there is our delight. When we like things in this world, we find much that might tempt us to sin and make us shameful of ourselves. To love God is to put Him first. If we love God with all our hearts, souls, minds, and strength, we won't let the things of this world tempt or shame us. Psalms 34:10 says, "Even strong young lions sometimes go hungry, but those who trust in the Lord will lack no good thing." Let God's glory be over all the earth and its inhabitants. Amen!

Through trials, difficulties, and any other pain that the evils of this world put in your path, you can run from state to state, city to city, job to job, or even church to church. Until you submit yourself to God's leadership, your past will follow you. Satan's mission is to hold us tethered to our past and keep us from trusting and believing our Lord and Savior. Submission to God is a must for transformation, and once God starts to work on your heart, a change is going to come. James 4:7 says, "Submit yourselves, then, to God. Resist the devil, and he will flee from you." Lord, thank You for forgiving me. Amen.

To backslide is to relapse in bad ways or error, and also to know the right thing to do but fail to do so. This happens because we have temporary faith, or false faith. Human beings, under the pressures of this world, adopt false values that cause us to temporarily disown the word of God. When we trust in our worldly abilities, this is where we fall. We come to Jesus for help so let Him take the wheel, and we should sit back and enjoy the ride. But by any chance you find yourself drifting away, turn back immediately and go to Hebrews 3:12–14. Once you start back, knowing and believing that Christ is the only way to salvation, this is called saving faith. Thank God for Jesus!

DON'T BE TRICKED BY DOUBT!

To doubt is to be uncertain of belief or opinion. Some people say that some doubt can be useful. In my opinion, it's only when talking about things of this world. Have you ever looked up an alternative to doubt? Doubt is used to trick us from obeying God, and once doubt is placed in our mind, we can never be at peace until we spend more time with His word, inviting the Holy Spirit into our hearts. We all know when God is speaking to us because His direction will be apparent, He will never tell you to sin or go against the teaching of His word; trusting in God's word will eliminate all doubt. Matthew 21:21 says, "Then Jesus told them, 'I tell you the truth, if you have faith and don't doubt, you can do things like this and much more. You can even say to this mountain, 'May you be lifted up and thrown into the sea,' and it will happen." Amen.

To Err Is Human, to Forgive Divine

This is my opinion, and I am not trying to change anything that is biblically written. In the world today we are so fixed on what title we have instead of being a genuine child of God. We can be confident that God knows our heart, so it doesn't matter what label we put on ourselves. Many are called, but few are chosen! The reason I say this is because I have been looking into the difference between a disciple and a Christian. To me, they are not synonymous because a disciple physically and personally believed and followed Jesus Christ. In my point of view, it means talking the talk and walking the walk. Being a Christian, on the other hand, means relating to or professing Christianity or its teachings. Many of us, as Christians, believe in Jesus Christ, but when it comes to walking the walk, we refer to our own understanding, not that of Christ. I understand that some titles are crucial when it comes to leading people to Christ not for us to be noticed by man. I was led to Matthew 23:1–12.

Resist Those Defilers!

There is a true trinity and a worldly trinity. Therefore, go and make disciples of all nations, baptizing them in the name of the Father and the Son and the Holy Spirit. Teach these new disciples to obey all the commands I have given you. And be sure of this: I am with you always, even to the end of the age. Now there is a trinity of defilers by which many hopeful lives have been spoiled, i.e., the world, the flesh, and the devil. God alone can teach us how to overcome the evils of these defilers. We must stay armored up in God's word! Submit yourselves, therefore, to God. Resist the devil, and he will flee from you. Amen.

GIVE AS CHRIST GAVE!

We say that we love God, but in our hearts and minds, there's a different story. Take a moment to think of the last sacrifice you made with no expectation of getting something in return. It's time to realize that God knows all, sees all, and is all, so let's take up the cross and give as Christ gave with no hesitation. "Do not withhold good from those who deserve it when it's in your power to help them. If you can help your neighbor now, don't say, 'Come back tomorrow, and then I'll help you'" (Proverbs 3:27–28). What's treasured here on earth will have no value in heaven. Amen!

THE GOOD SHEPHERD'S VOICE!

How do we know if it's God's voice we hear, or our flesh, or the devil? More than likely God communicates through the Bible, and His word is the light of our path. We should also pray and ask God to make His will clear, and when we pray, let no doubt enter our mind and believe by faith that the voice you hear is telling you something that is the Lord's Gospel. Our faith in God should automatically let us know whose voice we are hearing because God's voice will never tell us to do anything sinful. When we mistake the other two voices for God's voice, expect nothing good to happen. Get to know the Good Shepherd's voice!

Wake Up, Everybody!

Have you ever felt that a sermon was directed at you as if someone had told the preacher about your business? Most of the time we give the praise to the preacher. When this happens, it is our blessed Lord taking us by the hand to lead us back to Him. Humans think they can provide a safe place in the world by not trusting in God's holy word, but our God knew this from long ago that's why He confuses us, and from this day we are not able to understand each other. The time is now to stop following the lies of humans and go to the word of God, which was left here for us to follow. There are people who hear the true word but don't understand it. This makes them lean toward people's lies more than to the true love of God. Amen.

SOMEBODY'S WATCHING YOU!

We cannot act or speak in ways that are pleasing to the flesh and expect positive results. Nonbelievers wait for the moment when they can catch a Christian doing things that are not pleasing to God, so always ask yourself in all you do, "Am I doing what pleases God?" If you are, say to them, "Follow my example, as I follow the pattern of Christ," and watch them flee from your presence.

Who and What Do You Fear?

About three years ago I started writing devotionals about what I've lived through and how God's word kept me. As I got deeper into writing the devotionals, a fear came over me like a ton of bricks. I feared what people would say about me, i.e., what is he doing, he is the biggest sinner I know, what does he know about God, and much more. I slacked off on writing because of the fears I had, and I thought that all of my energy for writing was lost until I read Galatians 1:10: "Obviously, I'm not trying to win the approval of people, but of God. If pleasing people were my goal, I would not be Christ's servant." And by keeping God's will, nothing is lost. Lose it, and all is gone. Oh yeah, it's not what I know about God; it's what He knows about me! Amen.

WHO DO YOU REALLY FEAR?

Are there times when you want to hear a song or have a glass of wine or even watch a movie, but your pastor or some member of your church is around, so you put it off until they have left? Our all-knowing God can see all that goes on here on earth and in heaven. So why would we hide from people what God can see? It is foolish to think that we should fear people more than God. How can we expect Him to help us if we show more respect to humans than our Lord and Savior? When someone says he or she loves all people, but there are some whom he or she can't help because they sin, remember Jesus Christ laid down His life for all. This is how we know what true love is. People only want favor according to worldly standards, which are temporary, but the support of God is everlasting to everlasting, and his love is with those who fear Him, and His salvation extends to the children's children of those who obey His commandments. (Psalms 103:17–19)

Only God Can Give The All Clear!

I would always say, "I have faith in God," until I spoke to Him and asked Him to show me all the ways I had failed Him. The first thing that came to mind as I prayed was that I have more faith in myself than in my Lord and Savior. When a catastrophe hits, the first thing out of my mouth is I have to do this or that—the key is "I." When God calms the storm, I start to give Him praise, not before or during the storm but after God gives the all clear. I have work to do! I must remember that not one word has failed of all God's good promises.

It's me, oh Lord, standing in the need of prayer!

Is Your Prayer Request in Line with God?

Sometimes I pray for things and ask God to grant my prayer request, but as time passes by, and I don't see or hear from God about my petition, I start to wonder if He even listened to my prayer. I'm sure this happens to others as well. When you are faced with such a dilemma, ask yourself, "Is the prayer request I seek in line with the will of God?" or "Is this my top priority?" Sometimes our prayers to God can be selfish and one-sided. Also ask yourself, "Am I ready to handle the request that I seek?" If I counted all the blessings I have received, this would be a very long book that started in the late 1950s. God knows what's best for us and a lot better than we do. Somewhere in the instruction manual He left is the answer to all of our prayers. I found my answers in Matthew 7:11, Psalms 25:12, Romans 8:26–27, and Philippians 2:13.

I Helped Put Jesus on the Cross!

I would like everyone who reads this message to think of the worst hardship they ever faced, such as loss of a job, a crumbling relationship, mental or physical abuse, or betrayal—whatever you can think of adding to this list. Then think of what Jesus went through—the most painful torture and death you could imagine. Jesus rose from the dead! Now, with all the hardship you can think of, do you believe that our God, who healed the sick and raised the dead, can't handle your difficulty? No challenge you face is a match for our God! We must lay down all our burdens before God and then watch Him defeat all of our fears.

AS YOU WANT DONE TO YOU!

When you become a born-again Christian, you always worry about trying to be perfect and not sinning against God. There's good news and bad news. The bad news is that we can never be free of sin as long as we walk this earth, but the good news is God will always love you. He wants us to be obedient, and He doesn't like us any less when we mess up. Don't get it twisted; this is not a free pass to feel it is okay to hurt others and go against the word of God. We must repent and with a heartfelt apology. We cannot just say, "I'm sorry," or think it's okay because "I will be forgiven now that I'm a born-again Christian." When others sin against you, is "I'm sorry" good enough for you to forgive them? Don't forget that we will all be judged. As old or new Christians work hard to settle your case out of court by the word of God and showing love and respect to others. If you find yourself bordering the line of disobedience to the word of God, here's what I do: (1) go to scripture and (2) ask myself what Jesus would do!

Grace and peace.

WOULD JESUS BE PROUD OF ME?

I always thought that to be a true Christian and make Jesus proud, I had to follow the lead of other church-going Christians. Not to put anyone on the spot, but they are probably, like me, just doing what they were taught. Today we must listen for the whisper of God's voice and communicate with Him daily because most people mean well when they turn God's Gospel into their law and alter His holy word. Let's not make life-changing decisions based on our reasoning because disaster will be unavoidable without God's input. Be watchful of Satan while you pray, and make sure it's God's whisper you hear and not the evil one hollering to rush you into his trap. If you have a problem trying to distinguish between the two, ask what Jesus would do! Jesus would be proud if we believe and trust Him in every part of our lives and place our heart and mind entirely on God to lead us to what's best. Even a sinner's prayer is heard by God! Amen.

Search Me, Lord!

How many times have you asked someone to pray for you, and nothing changed? If you have asked God already, what in the world could anyone else do? Realize it or not, you are not trusting in God when you invite others to speed up His process. We serve an on-time God who doesn't need help from people in this world to fix his work. Don't misunderstand what I'm saying. There is nothing wrong with prayers sent up for you by others, but after you make your request to God, what can anyone do better than Him? Our problem is we can't see or ignore the carnality and iniquities in our way, and this is when we ask God to search us to find and change any wrong that He sees in us. "Search me, O God, and know my heart; test me and know my anxious thoughts. Point out anything in me that offends you, and lead me along the path of everlasting life" (Psalms 139:23–24).

FALSE PROMISES BEFORE GOD

When you find yourself in a situation that seems unbearable, be very careful before making a vow to God. It is unwise to commit yourself and make a promise to God without thinking it through. We know all too well that we can barely keep promises we make to each other. We disappoint our Lord God enough with our false bravado, and there is no need to add insult to injury by making promises hurriedly. Before making your next vow to God, read the promise Jephthah made in Judges 11:30–40. Let's make sure that any oath we make to God is in His will, and it will not make us say or do anything to keep us from the glory of God. In the flesh, we cannot trust; in God, we can!

THE TRUTH MAY HURT,
but Eventually It Will Set You Free!

Would you rather have someone preach to you about things that sound good or preach the real word of God and shame the devil? Most of us find it hard to hear the truth about ourselves; more than likely we want to hear something to pet our ego. Be very careful of anyone who is always swelling your head with false facts, no matter what you do; this makes sinning easier. False prophets will tell you things that seem right for the moment, but a true disciple of Christ will speak the truth that will last a lifetime. You will know when you are keeping company with false teachings. Your Bible reading will be abandoned, and your prayer life will grow dim, so let us not be afraid to hear the truth because the little hurt we feel will help us to learn more about being righteous. Psalm 1:6 says, "For the Lord watches over the way of the righteous, but the way of the wicked leads to destruction."

KEEP YOUR FAITH IN GOD
THROUGH GOOD TIMES AND BAD

The book of Job is one of my favorite books of the Bible. Job not only lost everything he had, but he also had to lose himself, yet he never said anything against God. If this were to happen to someone in the world today, it would be complicated to keep faith in God. As long as we think we can handle our lives alone, there is no room for God's blessings. To lose yourself, you must give up all your worldly behaviors; put God above all your earthly treasures; and let all of your boasting be about Christ our Lord, not about you as if you made it thus far on your own. Do you think you can give up the way you are living and let the word of God direct your path? Because the only way to find God is through losing your ways of this world. Philippians 4:19 says, "And my God will supply every need of yours according to his riches in glory in Christ Jesus."

Do You Love Your Status More Than God?

It's sad to watch people of today follow a sinner as if there is nothing wrong in doing so. It is ungodly to follow a wrathful person to keep your position because if we are careless of other people's sins, it won't be long before we become negligent of our sins. Psalms 26:4–5 says, "I do not spend time with liars or go along with hypocrites. I hate the gatherings of those who do evil, and I refuse to join in with the wicked." Proverbs 13:20 says, "Walk with the wise and become wise; associate with fools and get in trouble."

Let us sing praises to God out loud for the instructions He left us!

Do Your Trials Build Character?

Instead of fretting over all your past heartache, we should look at the blessings that we receive. I'm sure the blessings outweigh the anguish that your heart holds. We can never truly understand Christ's sacrifice for our sins until we are impoverished and stop our self-pity. As Christians, we should know that grief or sorrow should help us grow in faith, and we should use such experiences to learn that our situations are nothing compared to Christ's suffering. So let's look at any problem that may occur, and they will. Then see what we can take from them and focus on what we can learn to help build our character. We may endure many trials for a little while, for these trials make us partners with Christ in His suffering. Read 1 Peter 1:6–7, 1 Peter 4:12–16, and 2 Corinthians 1:8–10. God's instructions are enough to build your life on, without anything added!

Have You Ever Blamed God for What Happens in Life?

Do you recall saying or hearing, "He (or she) was a beautiful person. Why would God let something like this happen to them?" We may think we know someone, but in reality, we have no clue what this person may have done to deserve the hardship that he or she faces. Romans 3:10–12 says that no one is righteous—no, not one. No one understands; no one is seeking God. All have turned away; all have become useless. No one does good, not a single one. This is the devil's plan to have you blame God for what happens to others. If God says live, the devil says evil, and this is how things are turned backward to keep us confused. Don't let anyone or anything separate you from God's love! The evil one wants us to focus on all the bad when God wants us to remember all the blessings. It's much easier to count the bad things because they don't happen as often as blessings. The moral of this story is in James 4:7: "Submit yourselves, then, to God. Resist the devil, and he will flee from you."

Lord, Lead Me Along My Way!

By no means do I think I'm an expert on the Bible, nor do I like mixing religion with politics, but after reading 1 Samuel 8, I thought about what is going on in the world today. People have a way of thinking that humans are able to do more than God. We must be cautious when asking someone other than God to lead us and giving power to the unrepentant. Even though we all fall short of the glory of God, we cannot follow a nonbeliever in the word of God. A time will come when someone lets us down, and we will ask God to comfort us because of such a leader. God will not answer until we learn that there is no one greater than God, whom we rejected to please a man or woman. God will never be dishonest or pervert justice, and He will always keep his promise. Here is a short and sweet prayer we should keep in mind: Oh, Lord our God, if we ask anything that is not on the authority of your will, please have mercy on us and decline our request in Jesus's name.

Don't Lose Sight of True Worship

Church on Sunday and Bible study on Wednesday—this is like the sacrifices made back in the day. On the outside, it looks like true religion—what is going on inside your heart, mind, and soul—but can you say in your heart that you have expressed a lifestyle of holiness? Can we say we are in fellowship for the love of God or for our bragging rights? People who celebrate their worldly possessions usually find themselves ashamed of all their gloating. God is not impressed with our ceremonies and offers because they cannot wipe away our sins. Some people are willing to give up sinning but not the offenses that are excusable in the eyes of the world. Isaiah 1:16 says, "Wash yourselves and be clean! Get your sins out of my sight. Give up your evil ways." God is looking for us to worship Him in spirit and truth, not traditions.

REVELATION 21:3–8

And I heard a loud voice from the throne saying, "Look! God's dwelling place is now among the people, and he will dwell with them. They will be his people, and God himself will be with them and be their God. He will wipe every tear from their eyes. There will be no more death or mourning or crying or pain, for the old order of things has passed away."

He who was seated on the throne said, "I am making everything new!" Then he said, "Write this down, for these words are trustworthy and true."

He said to me: "It is done. I am the Alpha and the Omega, the Beginning and the End. To the thirsty I will give water without cost from the spring of the water of life. Those who are victorious will inherit all this, and I will be their God and they will be my children. But the cowardly, the unbelieving, the vile, the murderers, the sexually immoral, those who practice magic arts, the idolaters and all liars—they will be consigned to the fiery lake of burning sulfur. This is the second death."